INDIAN NAMES
FACTS AND GAMES

FOR

CAMP FIRE GIRLS

BY

FLORENCE M. POAST

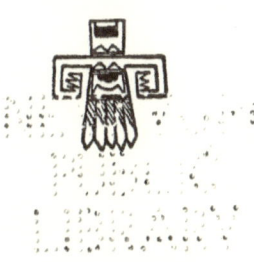

WASHINGTON
1916

CONTENTS.

Pueblo Water Carrier

The Indians　As all children know, when Columbus discovered the New World he thought he had found India by a new route, so when he described the natives to Queen Isabella and King Ferdinand he called them "Indios," which in the Spanish language means "Indians." Although the natives were not really Indians at all, the name has clung to them ever since, and by this name they will probably be known forever.

Applied to the Indians by some white people are a number of nicknames which should never be used in any way. It is disrespectful and unrefined to speak of an Indian man as "a big buck," or of his wife as a "squaw," and the term "Redskin" should also be forgotten. "Savage" is another name for the American Indian which, while not disrespectful, should not be used too freely. All Indians are not savages by any means; indeed many white people are inferior to some Indians in their ideals of right dealing, and in other ways.

While to our boastful ideas of civilization the Indian may appear as *savage*, a study of history shows us that the Indian has endured great injustice at the hands of his white brother.

It has been shown that the rascality of one white man or another was at the bottom of most so-called "Indian atrocities," while the wrongs suffered by the Indians are so well known that fair-minded white people feel very much ashamed of their treatment. Records left by traders and scouts of the early days even show that miners and others of the days of 1849 used often to go out hunting the Indians and shooting them down without provocation, just as they would shoot jack-rabbits.

Much has been written regarding the cruelty and treachery of the Indians, but it should be remembered that they met the first white men who landed on their shores with dignity and kindness. Not until they had been dealt with treacherously did they become "treacherous." The Indians' desire for revenge when once they had been injured, and the swiftness with which they wrought it, made them appear more cruel, perhaps, than they really were. Indians are usually honest, and their admiration for the white man whom they know to "talk straight" (will not lie) knows no bounds.

Many theories have been advanced in regard to the origin of the Indians, but to the present time no entirely satisfactory solution of the problem has been found, although it is now generally believed that they came from Asia by way of Bering Strait and Alaska thousands of years ago.

Regarding the population of the Indians, Mr. James Mooney, of the Bureau of American Ethnology, who has made a special study of the subject, estimates that at the time of the discovery of America there were probably 820,000 Indians north of Mexico alone, of whom 248,000 lived east of the Mississippi River. In 1915 the Indian Office gave a total Indian population for the United States, exclusive of Alaska, of 333,000. This number includes Indians of all degrees of mixed blood; in fact, it includes almost all persons who claim any Indian blood at all. Probably fewer than half this number are really pure-blood Indians.

With respect to Indian customs, these vary with each tribe according to the conditions under which they live. The marriage ceremony among the Sioux Indians of the northern plains, for example, was entirely different from that of the Seminoles of Florida. Some tribes bury their dead, others place the dead in little houses above the ground; some Indians burn their dead, others put the bodies in trees to protect them from wild animals. In some tribes the dead are laid with the head toward the east; others bury them in a sitting position. Possibly the only custom common to all Indians in this respect was that of burying with the dead such personal belongings as the pipe, tobacco, bow and arrows, or gun, blankets, small trinkets and ornaments of all kinds, and usually vessels of food and water, in order that the spirit of the dead might be properly provided on its long journey to the future world. The

Indian believed that each thing that occupied an important place in his life possessed a spirit the same as man, so that it was the spirits of the pipe, tobacco, bow and arrow, blanket and food and water that accompanied the dead, not the material things themselves. Sometimes the horse and the dog of a warrior were killed at his grave, and often his wife cut off her hair, smeared her face with charcoal, and cut her body until the blood flowed. It must be remembered, however, that customs of all kinds varied from tribe to tribe, so that what is true of one group of Indians is not necessarily true of another.

Zuni Sacred Butterfly

Language of The Indians Many people think of the Indians as speaking *one* language. This is very far from the truth. There are hundreds of tribes north of Mexico alone, and of the known languages there are more than three hundred! Some of these languages are very musical, while many others are almost unpronounceable by the English tongue. A few of the more pleasing languages are those of the Cherokee, the Seminole, the Creek, the Seneca and other Iroquois languages of New York and Canada; many of the Siouan languages of the northern plains and mountains, such as the Crow, Dakota, and Omaha; a few of the Algonquian languages, among which are the Chippewa, Delaware, Blackfoot, and Potawatomi; the language spoken by the Pawnee, and some of the languages of the Pueblo Indians of the Southwest.

Zuni Sacred Butterfly

Written Language

The Indians north of Mexico had no written language. As a rule, knowledge of historical events was handed down from generation to generation by word of mouth, although a few notable historic events were recorded by rock carvings, called pictographs, or by designs in wampum or shell beads, or were painted on animal skins or scratched on birch-bark. The first attempt at educating the American Indian to read and write his own language was made in 1665 by Father Leclerc, who invented a syllabary called "Micmac hieroglyphics," which was improved by Father Kauder in 1866. Many syllabaries are based on the Cree syllabary, or Evans syllabary, invented by the Reverend James Evans, a Methodist missionary in the Hudson's Bay region, in 1841, who adapted it from the shorthand systems current at that time. The most remarkable of all syllabaries is that known as the Cherokee alphabet, invented about 1821 by an uneducated half-blood Cherokee Indian named Sequoya; it first contained eighty-two syllables, later eighty-six were represented. Sequoya gained his idea from an old spelling-book, though the characters do not at all correspond to their English sounds. It was first used for printing in 1827, and has been in constant use since for correspondence and for various literary purposes among the Cherokee Indians. Sequoya's alphabet is given on the following page.

12

Cherokee Alphabet

Sounds represented by vowels:

a as *a* in *father*, or short as *a* in rivals.
e as *a* in *hate*, or short as *e* in *met*.
i as *i* in *pique*, or short as *i* in *pit*.
o as *aw* in *law*, or short as *o* in *not*.
u as *oo* in *fool*, or short as *u* in *pull*.
v as *u* in *but*, nasalized.

Consonant Sounds:

g nearly as in English, but approaching to k.
d nearly as in English, but approaching to t.
h, k, l, m, n, q, s, t, w, y, as in English.

13

While the Indians north of Mexico had no written language at the time of the discovery of America, we should not forget the remarkable hieroglyphic writing of the Maya Indians of Central America and Yucatan. Some of the monuments of this people bear inscriptions, in curious hieroglyphics, that have been found to record dates that go back a period of two thousand years.

Penn Treaty Belt of Wampum

Symbolism There seems to be as much misunderstanding with respect to symbolism as there is in regard to the languages of Indians. Many persons seem to have the idea that the Indians had not only a symbolic meaning for every object or action known to them, but that all Indians understood them alike. This is by no means the case.

Little has been published on the subject of the symbolism of the Indians, for the reason that this is a study which is not yet complete. In the hundreds of different tribes north of Mexico there may be various meanings for the same symbol. It is true that the Indians symbolize only that object or phenomenon of nature which occupies an important place in their lives. For example: The Pueblo Indians of the Southwest are an agricultural people who live in an arid country. To them it is of great importance that they should have rain in season (rainfall is a phenomenon of nature); thus they sometimes symbolize the rain-cloud as a triangle with the life-giving rain falling from it. On the other hand, some of the Indians of the Plains might read this symbol as meaning the foot of a bear and thus would look for the near presence of the bear itself, while certain Indians of the Northwest coast, who live by fishing, would interpret the triangle as the dorsal fin of the killerwhale.

15

From this example it will be seen that all Indians do not read symbols alike, nor is there a symbol for every flower, bird, or animal known to them, or for such abstract virtues as honor, goodness, and kindness.

Dragon-fly Totem

Sign Language The sign language is frequently confused with symbolism. The sign language is a system of gestures used by some Indians for communicating with tribes speaking different languages. A symbol is an object or an action that conveys a meaning distinct from the actual meaning conveyed by the object or action.

There is evidence that a sign language was once used in the eastern part of the United States, in the Canadian Northwest, and in Mexico, but it appears that no such system was used west of the Rocky mountains excepting by the Nez Percé Indians, who frequently made excursions into the prairies in pursuit of game, and thus came into intimate contact with the Plains tribes. So the sign language as known today belongs to the tribes between Missouri river and the Rocky mountains and from the Saskatchewan river in Canada to the Rio Grande. This vast region, extending two thousand miles north and south, is commonly known as the Great Plains, and the tribes that lived therein are collectively called Plains Indians. This great body of Indians was made up of a large number of tribes speaking different languages, but as all roamed the plains either on hunting or war expeditions, they were continually brought into friendly meeting or hostile collision. This constant association resulted in a highly developed system of gestures as a means of

17

communication which, for all ordinary purposes, almost equaled a spoken language. This was the origin of the sign language. It is said that the Crow, Cheyenne, and Kiowa Indians are more expert in its use than any other tribes, and that for ease and grace of movement a conversation between a Cheyenne and a Kiowa Indian is the very poetry of motion.

Hopi "Canteen" made of Basketry Water-proofed with Pitch

Signals The system of long-distance signals used by many Indians tribes may be regarded as supplementary to the sign language. These signals were in greatest use by the Plains Indians of the middle-western and southwestern United States, where the view was unobstructed, often for many miles, and the air very clear. In swampy regions, where the air was cloudy from the warm climate, and the view was often interrupted by forests, long-distance signals were not in such common use. These signals were ordinarily conveyed by smoke in the daytime, fire by night, or by the movements of men either on foot or on horse. Their purpose was generally to indicate danger or the presence of game. The drum was also used to call people together on ceremonial occasions. In forest regions signals were also made by bending a twig, cutting the bark of trees, piling up stones, or carving rude pictures on rocks.

A Hopi Drawing of a Ceremony

Totems The word "totem" is a corruption of the term *ototeman*, which means "his brother-sister kin" in Chippewa and related Algonquian languages. Among the Indians there are many tribes which have groups of persons called "clans" or "gentes." In the clan the child takes its family

name and inherits property from the mother, while in the gens it takes its name and inherits property through the father. These clans are usually named for some animal, bird, or plant, such as deer, bear, raven, turtle, buffalo, eagle, hawk, corn. An Indian belonging to the Bear clan might meet another Indian who was a

Killerwhale Totem

total stranger to him, yet if the stranger drew the rude outline of a bear, or indicated in any other way the clan to which he belonged, the Indian would greet him as a brother, because the two belonged to the same clan. So strongly was this relationship regarded that a man could not marry a woman belonging to the same clan or gens as himself, as that would be the same as marrying his own sister.

Raven Totem

Many people have thought that when an Indian

20

drew the rude outline of some animal, he was making his personal mark or signing his name. This is not true. He was drawing the emblem, or totem, of the clan to which he belonged, which was his way of saying "I am a member of the Deer clan," or whatever clan it might be.

Frog Totem

Totem Poles   Totem poles are carved cedar poles erected by the Indians inhabiting the Northwest coast from Vancouver Island, British Columbia, to Alaska. Poles that stand in the open in front of the houses are three or more feet wide at the base, and sometimes more than fifty feet high. The very wealthy members of the tribes sometimes had totem poles that stood inside their houses; these poles were not very large and they stood in the middle of the house directly behind the fireplace, marking the seat of honor. Smaller totem poles were used as grave-posts.

These Northwest-coast Indians perform a great winter ceremony the native name of which, in one of the languages of the region, is *patshatl*, which means "gift" or "giving." This name, being rather awkward for the English tongue, was corrupted by white people into "potlatch," and this is the name by which the ceremony is now popularly known. Potlatches are always marked by great feasts at which quantities of goods, commonly blankets, are given away by the one who gives the ceremony. Sometimes the host gives away everything he owns, with the exception of his house, but

Totem Pole of the Kwakiutl Indians

22

by this generosity he gains great respectability among his people, and when someone else gives a potlatch, he receives his share with interest, so that often in the end the giver is richer than he was before.

It was during these potlatches that the totem poles were erected. The trunks of the trees from which they were carved were cut down amid songs and dancing, then rolled into the water and towed to the village. Regular carvers were employed to cut the designs, and these men were always paid very handsomely. Among some tribes the carvings represented some story of what the man who was erecting the pole had done, or a tribal myth, while among others they depicted the traditions of the owner of the house, and hence were a kind of family tree. Grave-posts usually bore only the crest owned by the family of the deceased.

Owing to the pressure of civilization on the Indians from all sides, the custom of erecting totem poles is now dying out.

It should be borne in mind that totem poles and totems are not related in any way. A totem is the official emblem of a clan or gens, while a totem pole may be a memorial column representing an incident in the life of the man who erected the pole, or it may be merely the representation of a tribal myth.

Fire-making One thing which all Camp Fire Girls should study and practice is the method of producing fire without the aid of matches. Following are descriptions and illustrations of two of the simplest means the Indians had of making fire.

Hand-drill Two pieces of cedar wood are best for this purpose, though dry, "punky" wood of any kind is suitable. The larger piece is the socket, or hearth, and the smaller piece, which should be somewhat harder than the hearth, is called the spindle. This simple apparatus is called the "twirled hand-drill," and the process of using it is the simplest as well as the most primitive means of procuring fire. A quantity of "tinder," that is, very fine slivers of dry wood, should be used to make the flame after the spark is produced. The illustration shows the method of operating this drill.

1. A shallow depression is made in the hearth in order to hold in place the end of the spindle. A groove is cut down the side of the hearth from this depression, to accommodate the wood powder which will be ground off.

Making Fire with the Hand-drill

2. Take the spindle by its upper end between the

24

palms of the hands; insert the lower end in the depression of the hearth; twirl rapidly with a strong downward pressure; the hands, which necessarily move downward through the combined pressure and the backward and forward movement, must be re-returned quickly to the top of the spindle without allowing the air to get under the lower end of the spindle.

Flame is never directly produced in this manner; the spark or "coal" must be placed in contact with the tinder and fanned into flame. This is a smoky process, but with practice one becomes so expert that a flame can be produced in one minute or less.

Plowing Method For this method of making fire the implements are a short, cylindrical, pointed stick, called a "rubber," and a larger billet of wood, in which a groove is sometimes begun, called the "hearth". The rubber is

grasped between the hands, and, held at an angle, is projected to and fro along the groove of the larger stick, or hearth, upon which the operator kneels. At first the rubber is forced back and forth along the

Making Fire by the Plowing Method

groove for a space of six or seven inches; then, as

the wood begins to wear away, the movement is increased and the range shortened until, as the stick is moved with great rapidity, the brown dust ignites; then, as the tinder is applied, it is easily fanned into flame.   An expert operator can produce fire in this manner in a few seconds.

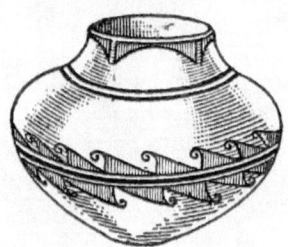

Pueblo Water Jar

Indian Homes It is common for people to think of a "wigwam" whenever they have the Indian in mind, as though all Indians lived in wigwams the year round. A few types of Indian dwellings will be mentioned:

A wigwam is not a tent, but an arbor-like or conical structure built over a shallow depression in the ground. In some localities

Winnebago Bark Wigwam

wigwams resemble hay-cocks. The framework of poles is covered with bark, rushes, or flags.

A tipi (tee'pee) is a circular dwelling made by setting poles at an angle in a circle about fifteen feet in diameter, tied together at the top, and covered with skins.

Nez Perce Skin Tipi

27

Other Indians built earth lodges by excavating a circle from thirty to sixty feet in diameter and a few feet deep, then erecting posts, across the top of which were laid heavy beams; across the beams were placed the trunks of long slender trees, which were covered with willow branches; on top of these was laid coarse grass tied in bunches, and the whole was covered with sods placed like shingles. The floor within was made hard and smooth by wetting and stamping many times. The doorway was covered with a skin.

Some of the natives of Alaska build earth lodges in similar fashion; others build their houses of whale-bone and stones; winter dwellings are built of ice by some of the Eskimo of the Arctic region.

The Northwest-coast Indians live in houses of wood. Some writers say that the genius of these Indians in erecting these wooden houses might well have placed them among the foremost builders of America. Great labor was expended in getting out the huge tree-trunks, and in carving the house and totem poles. Some of these dwellings were large enough to shelter several families.

The Pueblo (pway'blo) Indians of the Southwest build houses of adobes (ah do'bays, sun-dried bricks) or of stone. There are old pueblos or towns in this dry region which have been standing since before Columbus discovered America. The cliff-dwellings, built high up in the face of precipices, were occupied by the forefathers of the present Pueblo Indians as a defense against their enemies.

Zuni Pueblo, New Mexico

Other tribes of Indians in the southeastern part of the United States built dwellings of grass, or of palmetto leaves, which, when finished, looked like great beehives. The Wichita tribe. which formerly lived in Kansas but are now in Oklahoma, were noted for their grass houses.

Wichita Grass House

From this brief description it will be seen that all Indians did not live in wigwams; indeed some Indians never saw a wigwam.

29

Occupations of Women

Another often mistaken idea with regard to Indians is that the women are drudges and household slaves. Among the Indians of North America each sex had its own particular duties, which varied greatly according to the manner in which the tribe lived. It was the duty of the men of all tribes to protect and support their wives, children, and kindred, but it may easily be imagined that when tribes were at war the men had little time for anything else.

In tribes that lived by hunting and were much given to war, the warrior was frequently absent far from home on the chase or the warpath. These absences varied from weeks to months and sometimes as much as a year. Often hunters or warriors

Zuni Eating Bowl

traveled hundreds of miles and suffered great hardship; many times they were in danger of death through hunting and fighting, and of ill health through exposure and lack of food. In these long journeys it became necessary for the wife and the older children to do all the work pertaining to the care of the family and the home, in addition to the work which she shared in common with her husband. From being so frequently left alone the woman came to do much that she otherwise would

30

not have been required to do. When on the march the care of all camp outfits and family belongings fell to the woman. It was from seeing the women, assisted by their children, performing this heavy work that white people came to believe that Indian women were little better than slaves.

Among the Indians who live in permanent settlements, such as the agricultural Pueblo Indians of the Southwest, the women cultivate the gardens and help to care for the larger crops, carry water, make pottery, weave blankets, and care for the children; and, indeed, they perform a multitude of tasks. The men do most of the heavier farming, gather fuel, make moccasins and other articles of clothing for their wives and children, and help the women with the heavier part of the work of house-building, although the houses are built and owned by the women.

Hopi Baby Shoe

In fact, the work seems to be about as equally divided as possible under the circumstances.

The general work of Indian women may be classified as follows:

Gathering roots, seeds, and plants for future use. Preparing and cooking the food. Making dyes for coloring basketry and clothing. Carrying water. Gardening. Skin dressing. Weaving. Making pottery vessels and basketry.

31

Clothing The costumes of the American Indian women north of Mexico, taken as a whole, differed very little. As a rule they consisted of a long shirt-dress, belt, leggings, and moccasins. The hair was usually worn parted in the middle and hanging in a braid at each side of the face. Those tribes whose dress differed distinctly from all others were the Eskimo of the Northwest and the Pueblo Indians of the Southwest.

Hopi Maiden

Most people are familiar with the fur suits worn by the Eskimo men and women, but fewer are acquainted with the picturesque dress of the Pueblo women. This costume consists of a knee-length woolen dress made in the form of a blanket, the two ends sewed together; the garment is worn over the right shoulder and under the left, belted at the waist

32

with a very long sash, usually of red and green wool, fringed at the ends and tucked in (see frontispiece); for indoor use a cotton skirt extending to the knees and knitted leggings of yarn were worn. For gala occasions the leggings sometimes consist of an entire deerskin wrapped round from below the knee to ankle and forming part of the moccasins of the same material. The hair of the married women of the Pueblo Indians is worn slightly banged in front, and wrapped in two large coils back of the ears; the girls of the Hopi (one of the Pueblo tribes) wear their hair in two large whorls at the sides of the head. These whorls are in imitation of the squash blossom, which is the symbol of both purity and fertility. When the girls are married the whorls are taken down and the hair is worn as above described.

Ornament The Indians of all tribes were fond of personal adornment, which sometimes was carried to extreme. The women of some of the Eskimo tribes wore a ring in the nose; to the Indians of the Plains elk-teeth and bear-claws were very precious; while the Pueblo Indians still wear bracelets and rings of silver, and necklaces of silver, turquoise, and shell. All Indians are fond of bright colors.

Feathers Feathers as a means of decoration were used in many ways. Some tribes used them for ornamenting ceremonial costumes; others

33

wove them into their blankets; the Eskimo sewed little sprays of feathers into the seams of his clothing and bags. The quills of small birds and of porcupines were split and dyed and used for beautiful embroidery and for ornamenting bags and basketry.

Indian women never wore quill-feathers in their hair, though they are often seen thus decorated both in magazines and on the motion-picture screen. Feathers in the hair of an Indian man indicated war honors, which, of course, were not possible with women. Among the Chippewa Indians, if a man scalped an enemy he was permitted to wear two feathers in his hair; if he captured a wounded prisoner on the battlefield he was permitted to wear five. If Camp Fire Girls desire to wear an Indian headdress, a beaded band is not only becoming but true to Indian custom.

Chippewa Writing on Birch-bark

Indian Children When school children are studying their history on warm, lazy spring days, they are likely to say to themselves, "I wish I were an Indian!" particularly when they are reading about the natives of the West Indies where Columbus first caught a glimpse of the New World, or about Powhatan and Pocahontas. Children often have the idea that the life of the Indian is one long holiday, especially that of the Indian child. But

Indian children have their les-
sons to learn, just as white
children have, and at an early
age are instructed by their
elders, not only in hunting and
the household arts, but in the
traditions and religious ideas of
the tribe.   At about the age
of fifteen the boy bids farewell
to his childhood life and takes
up his duties as a man and

Indian Girl

a member of his tribe. The girls generally mature at an earlier age than the boys, and at thirteen years, in many tribes, they are ready to assume the duties of women. So, after all, the little white child has a much longer "play-time" than the Indian, as our girls and boys are usually looked on as being children until they are eighteen or twenty years of age.

Indian parents are devoted to their children. Among some tribes the father makes ready for the

35

coming of the little infant by preparing the wooden frame for its cradle, which is the child's portable bed until it is able to walk. After the frame of the cradle is made it is ornamented by the grandmother, or by some woman in the tribe noted for her expertness, with beads, quill-work, fringes, and bangles. Since the Indian no longer roams the country at will, as he did in the days of his forefathers, but lives on reservations in houses, much as white people live, the baby is kept in the cradle only when on a journey or when being carried about; the remainder of the time it rolls about on the ground or on the bed as much as it pleases. In primitive times, however, it was taken out of the cradle only to exercise its little limbs and stretch itself, then put back again. The cradle swung in the breeze on the limb of a tree, out of the way of poisonous snakes and harmful insects, while the mother worked near-by.

Little girls are their mothers' companions, and very early are taught all that pertains to the arts of home life, such as sewing, cooking, weaving, gathering medicinal roots and barks, and taking care of the smaller brothers and sisters. In fact, the care of the baby of the home is usually the first task learned by the little Indian girl, as she is its constant attendant while the mother is busy with her many household duties. In this way the eldest girl becomes versed in medicine; thus, if the mother were taken away, there would be "one who could help" in the household.

The life of the little Hopi girl of the Southwest is full of labor, such as few little white girls dream of; but even then she is happy, for the Hopi are a happy people, the women singing at their labors, the children singing at their play, and the men also singing as they work in the fields. Aside from caring for the babies, the little girls help their mothers to weave, to grind the corn which they make into bread, or, with the other children, to keep the birds from the crops. When the mother goes to carry water the little girl accompanies her, and if too small to carry a water-jar, she fills her little pottery canteen, which she carries up the steep and rocky trail four hundred feet high. And yet, with all her duties, the little Hopi girl has time to play with her dolls.

Fighting and quarreling among Indian children are almost unknown, and so well-behaved and obedient are they that it may be said an Indian child never needs to be punished.

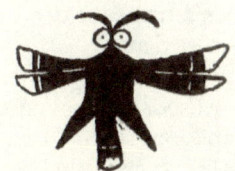

Southwestern Pottery Decoration

Naming of Children Without regard to language, the Indians north of Mexico may be divided into two classes—those with clan or gens organization, and those without (see page 20). In those tribes in which such organization exists, the manner of naming a child is sometimes an elaborate ceremony. Each clan had its own set of names, distinct from those of all other clans, and usually referring to the totems of the tribe. The children in these tribes are usually born into the use of certain names. While still infants, or at least very small, they frequently have no particular name, being called "child," "baby," or "girl," until they are old enough to take their tribal names. The names they are given at that time are used the remainder of their lives, although, as among white people, nicknames are common. The Iroquois tribes have sets of clan names which are used exclusively by members of each clan: there is a name for each period in life, classified as follows: boys' names, men's names, elder men's names, official names; girls' names, women's names, elder women's names, and official (women's) names.

Among those tribes which do not have a clan organization the methods of naming children differ, but as a rule the children receive two names, one at birth and the other when the boy or man has done something to distinguish him from his fellows. Among some tribes the child is named from some incident in connection with its birth: thus, if the sun coming up in the sky were the first thing the mother saw, the child might be named "Coming Sun," and this name would be used until he had distinguished himself either for skill or bravery, or for some meritorious action. A boy's father and mother usually addressed him all his life by his boyhood name. Generally the names of men and women differed, though not always. Indian girls' names frequently expressed whole sentences instead of a single word, as in the Yankton Sioux name, Wastewayakapiwin (Wah stay wah yah kah pee ween), "Woman who is pretty to look at." They were never named after such moral qualities as faith, hope, or charity, as is common among the white people, nor for garnets, opals, and the like, though in some tribes women have been named for flowers, as in the Iroquois term "Aweont" (ah way' ongt), meaning "It is a growing flower." The Indian girl would not be named simply "Rose," as a white girl is named, but she would be given a name which might mean "She is a beautiful rose," or "Rose Woman." Names for houses and canoes often followed those of families and clans, like personal names.

Eagle Totem

Dolls The little Indian girl, though early taught the arts of home life, is much like the little white girl when it comes to dolls, for, regardless of the

tribe to which she belongs, if she has no doll of her own she will fashion one of a corn-cob or a bundle of corn-husks, in much the same manner that a small white girl dresses a squash or a bundle of rags.   Sometimes the little Indian girl takes a puppy, and, wrapping it in a cloth, suspends it across her back

Doll of the Plains
Indians

in a sling, in imitation of her mother carrying her baby brother or sister in its cradle.

Indian parents, however, have the greatest affection for their children, and it would be a very poor family

Eskimo Dolls

indeed if the father could not find the time to carve a doll for his little daughter.

Away up in Eskimo-land where, in winter time, the people live in funny little houses made of ice,

40

called igloos, and the little girls wear fur suits so like those of their brothers that a stranger cannot tell them apart, the Eskimo father carves the dolls from ivory or bone. So well are they made that they will stand on their feet, much to the delight of the little girls.

Dolls were common among all tribes. Those used merely as playthings were often dressed quite finely, in accordance with the customs of the tribe, by the mother of the little girl, and often they were provided with little cradles and dishes made of pottery.

Among the Pueblo Indians of the Southwest were many dolls made in imitation of their various deities,

Hopi Doll and Cradle

which are represented by men and women in the great religious dances. These dolls are made by priests in the kivas (kee'vahs), or ceremonial rooms, while they are preparing to take part in the ceremonies which sometimes continue for several days, and on the morning of the last day the dolls are presented to the little girls. These dolls are made usually of cottonwood, and are so carved and painted as to represent

41

in miniature the elaborate head-dress, mask, body, and costume of particular deities. In this way the young become familiar with the complicated and symbolic masks, ornaments, and garments worn in performing the religious rites of the tribe. The dolls were never worshipped, but travelers have often mistaken them for idols.

In the Southwest and the extreme North little figures or dolls are made for use in ceremonies in which mythic ancestors or dead relatives are remembered. Among the Eskimo there is a festival in which small dolls are used to represent the dead, and food is prepared and eaten in the presence of these little figures in memory of the time when those represented by them were living.

Hopi Doll, made of wood and painted

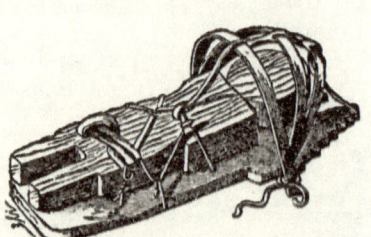

Hopi Doll and Cradle

Games Investigators among the Indians have been surprised to find so many games in use by them. These games, which are all of native origin, are divided into two great groups —games of skill, and games of chance, or gambling games. Notwithstanding all these games, the Indian girls have few amusements aside from playing with dolls or some of the various ball-games. The older women play some of the gambling games, but as these are not of interest to Camp Fire Girls they are not listed here. The games following are distinctly women's games, while battledore and shuttlecock is a universal child's game.

Northwest Coast Battledore and Shuttlecock

Double Ball This game is played with two balls fastened together by a cord about five inches long; the balls are thrown and caught by sticks with a hook or a fork at the end; the sticks may be any length between twenty-six inches and six feet. The bases are two poles set from three hundred to four hundred feet apart, though in some tribes they are set at a distance of a mile apart. The object of the game is to get the

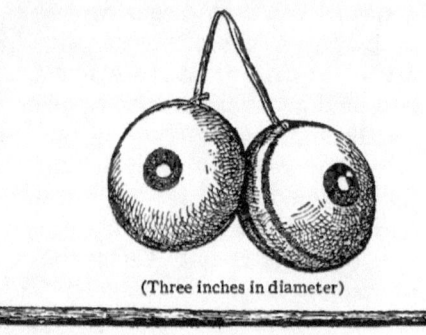

(Three inches in diameter)

(Length, 26 inches to 6 feet. They may also be slightly hooked or bent at the end, if preferred.)

Double-ball and Sticks

ball over the opponents' base-line, or to take one's own ball home, as in the American game of "shinny."

The balls may be of any shape and weighted with sand, or made from billets of wood.

Hand and Foot Ball
(Six inches in diameter)

Hand and Foot Ball

This game is played with a large leather ball, which is let fall first on the foot and then on the knee, again throwing it up and catching it, thus keeping it in motion for a

44

length of time without letting it fall to the ground. The one who keeps it up longest, wins.

Ball and Stick Game The Choctaw Indian girls have a game in which they take a small stick (or any small object) off the ground after having thrown a small ball into the air which they catch again, having picked up the stick. (This game corresponds to the little white girls' game of "jacks".)

Woman's Foot Ball This game may be played by two or more persons. If four persons play together, they stand in the form of a square. Each pair of players has a ball, which is thrown or driven back and forth across the square.

The ball is thrown upon the ground, midway between the players, so that it shall bound toward the oppo- site one. She strikes the ball down and back toward her part-

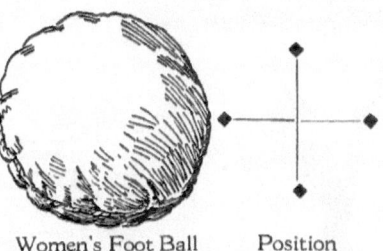

Women's Foot Ball   Position
(Seven and one-half inches)

ner with the palm of her hand. Sometimes the ball is caught on the toe or hand and tossed up, then struck or kicked back toward the other side. The one who misses the least, or has fewer "dead" balls on her side, wins.

45

The Winnebago Indian girls play the game with a ball made of a light, soft object, such as a stuffed stocking-foot. This ball is placed on the toe, then while the player stands on the other foot the ball is kicked into the air a few inches, and as it falls it is caught on the toe and again kicked up. The object of the game is to send the ball up as often as possible without letting it fall to the ground. When one girl misses, the next takes her turn. The first to count one hundred (or any number decided on) wins the game.

Battledore and Shuttlecock   This game is played by both boys and girls. The Zuni children of New Mexico play with the shuttlecock only, which is made of woven cornhusks decorated with feathers and batted with the

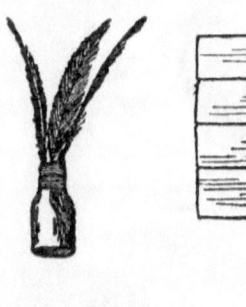

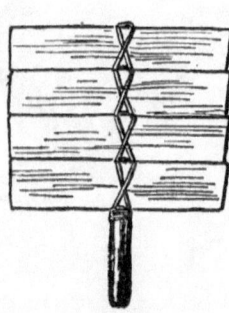

Shuttlecock
(3 inches high)

Battledore
(12 inches square)

Shuttlecock
(5 to 7 inches high)

46

palm of the hand. The children of the Northwest-coast Indians make a battledore of four slats of unpainted wood, and a shuttlecock of a piece of twig stuck with three feathers. The size of the battledore may be from twelve to fourteen inches, and the shuttlecock from three to seven inches in length. Two can play the game, or if there are many they stand in a circle and bat always toward the right, and in front of the body. The one who lasts longest wins.

Wichita Double Ball and Stick
(Length of Stick, 23 inches)

Indian Names for Camp Fire Girls In the section on Naming Indian Children it is shown that many tribes follow definite customs in naming their children. As white people follow no fixed rules for naming their children, the Indian names listed herein will be found to meet the needs of Camp Fire Girls as personal names, club and camp names, and canoe or boat names, in various Indian languages. It should be remembered that while these are the Indian names for the terms given, the Indians themselves would not necessarily use all of them as personal names without some explanatory suffix in addition. Included in this list, however, are a few typical Indian personal names; these are indicated by stars.

Many Indian languages are very difficult for the English-speaking tongue to pronounce; indeed there are numerous shades of sounds in some of the languages that the English ear fails to catch at all, and in this way many so-called Indian names have been recorded that are so far from correct that the Indian himself would not recognize the terms if he heard them spoken. Then, too, Frenchmen have written down Indian words in the French language; Germans in the German language, and Englishmen in the English language, and each has used characters to indicate sounds in his own language that perhaps might not exist in any of the others. Thus, one recorder might give the letter *a* the value of a in *cat;* another *a* as in *father,* and still another might give the letter *a* a sound resembling *u* as in *tub.* In order to avoid confusing the young people who use this book, by giving a complicated system of diacritical marks, the names have been given in simplified spelling with the pronunciation following in parentheses. In words without accents, all syllables should be given the same stress.

Hopi Basket

Personal Names

NATICK—*Massachusetts*

Chogan (cho'gahn)—Blackbird
Mishannock (mish an' nock)—Morning star
Tummunk (tum' munk)—Beaver
Weetomp (wee' tomp)—Friend; kinsman
Wohsumoe (woh' soo mo' ay)—Bright; shining
Wunnegen (wun' ne gen)—Good; desirable; pleas-
ing; handsome
Wuttaunin (wut' taw nin)—Daughter

ONONDAGA—*New York*

Awenhatagi (ah weng hah tah' gee)—Wild rose
Jiskaka (dji skah' kah)—Robin
Kaahongsa (kah a hong' sa)—Jack-in-the-pulpit
(Indian baby-cradle)
Kanawahaks (kah nah wah' hahks)—Cowslip (It
opens the swamps from blossoming in the spring)
Nakayagi (nah kah yah' gi)—Beaver
Oawensa (oh a weng' sah)—Sunflower
Osohada (oh so ha' dah)—White cedar (feather
leaf)
Oyongwa (oh yong' wah)—Golden rod
Skajiena (skah djee ay' nah)—Eagle (big claws)
Skennontonh (sken nong' tonh)—Deer
Takwahason (tahk wah hah' sone)—Flying squirrel

50

SENECA—*New York*

Awendea (ah weng day' ah)*—Early day
Aweinon (ah way ee' nong)*—Moving flowers
Aweogon (ah way' oh gon)*—Nothing but flowers
Aweont (ah way' ongt)*—Growing flower
Dewendons (day weng' dongs)*—It swings
Djaweondi (djah way' on dee)*—Beyond the flower
Ganonkwenon (gah nonk way' none)*—She is alert
Gaondawas (gah ong dah' ways)*—She shakes the
  trees

NARRAGANSETT—*Rhode Island*

Anekus (a nee' kus)—Ground squirrel; chipmunk
Moosquin (moos' kin)—A fawn
Chippanock (chip pah' nock)—The Pleiades
Kokokehom (ko ko' ke hom)—Large owl
Munnanock (mun na' nock)—Moon, or sun
Paupock (paw' pock)—Partridge
Sokanon (sock' a non)—Rain
Wequash (we' quash)—Swan
Wuskowhan (wus ko' whan)—Pigeon

DELAWARE—*Pennsylvania, New Jersey, New York,
  Delaware (later Ohio, Indiana, Kansas, Oklahoma, Texas)*

The vowels in this list of Delaware names take the short
sound (*a* as in hat; *e* as in met; *i* as in pin; *o* as in not; *u* as in
nut). As there are no accented syllables the words are
pronounced as spelled.

Chimalus—Bluebird
Cholena—Bird

51

Cholentit—Little bird
Nichantit—My little friend
Tipatit—Little chicken
Waselandeu—Clear sunshine
Wisawanik—Red squirrel
Woapasum—White sunshine
Woatwes—Flower
Wuligachis—Pretty little paw
Wulisso—Good; handsome; pretty
Zelozelos—Cricket

POWHATAN—*Virginia*

These names are from a vocabulary by William Strachey in his "Historie of Travaile into Virginia Britannia," written in 1611. The author's spelling has not been changed, and as there is no other historical authority for these words (the Powhatan language being extinct), they must be taken as they are.

Amonosoquath (ah mon' so quath)—Bear
Amosens (ah' mo sens)—Daughter
Arrokoth (ah' ro koth)—Sky
Asqueowan (ahs' kwee oh wahn)—Arrow
Assimoest (ahs' sih mo' est)—Fox
Cheawanta (chee ah wahn' tah)—Robin
Kikithamots (ki kith' ah mots)—The wind
Mahquaih (mah' quai)—A great wind
Manaang-gwas (mah nah ahng gwahs)—Butterfly
Matacawiak (mah tah kah wee' ak)—Pearl
Meightoram (my' to ram)—"A post"
Missanek (miss' ah neck)—Squirrel
Momuscken (mo mus' ken)—A mole

Monanaw (mo' nah naw)—Turkey

Nechaun (ne' chawn)—Child

Netab (ne' tahb)—"A friend—or the principal word of kindness")

Nonattewh (no' nat tooh)—Fawn

Opotenaiok (oh po tee nai' ok)—Eagle

Paskamath (pas' ka math)—Mulberries

Pussaqwembun (pus sa kwem' bun)—Rose

Qwannacut (kwan' na kut)—Rainbow

Qwanonats (kwan' oh nahts)—Wood pigeon

Raputtak (rap' put tack)—Arrowhead

Suckimma (suck' kim mah)—New moon

Tshecomah (she' ko mah)—Musselshell

Tsheship (she' ship)—Duck

Ussak (us' sack)—Crane

Wekowehees (we ko we' hees)—Hare

Woussicket (woo sick' et)—Running brook

Yapam (yah'' pam)—The sea

CHIPPEWA—*Michigan, Minnesota, Wisconsin, Illinois, and Ontario and Manitoba, Canada*

Anang (ah nahng')—Star

Anangons (ah nahn gons')—Little star

Ananidji (ah' nahn i dji')—Pearl

Bidaban (bid ah bahn')*—It begins to dawn

Debwewin (dabe weh win')—Truth

Enabandang (en' ah bahn dahng')—Dreamer

Inawendiwin (in' ah wen di win')—Friendship

Memengwa (mem en gwah)—Butterfly

Migisi (mi gi si')—Eagle
Namid (nah mid')—Dancer
Opitchi (o pit chee')—Thrush; robin
Wabanang (wah bah nahng')—Eastern star; morning star
Wabaningosi (wah' bah nin go si')—Snowbird
Wahwahtassee (wah' wah tas see')—Glow worm
Wawinges (wah win ges')—Skilful

MIAMI—*Wisconsin, Michigan. Illinois, Indiana, Ohio*

Ahsonzong (ah son' zong)—Sunshine
Metosanya (met oh san' yah)—Indian
Monjenikyah (mon jee ni kyah)—Big body
Onzahpakottek (ong zah pah kot' tek)—Yellow flower

CHEYENNE — *Minnesota; later, South Dakota, Nebraska, Montana, Colorado, Wyoming, Kansas, and Oklahoma.*

Hoimani (ho ee mah nee)—Lawmaker
Ihikona (ee hee' ko nah)—Industrious worker
Istas (ee' stahs)—Snow
Maishi (mah ee shee')—Robin-redbreast
Nisimaha (nee see mah hah')—My comrade
Otokson (oh toe' ksone)—Little stars
Wikis (wee kees')—Bird

CHEROKEE—*North and South Carolina, Georgia, Tennessee, Alabama, Kentucky, and Virginia*

Adsila (ad see' lah)—Blossom

Aginaliya (ah gee nah' lee yah)—My true friend

Awinita (ah wee nee' tah)—Young deer

Ayasta (ah yas' tah)*—The spoiler

Ayita (ah yi' tah)—Worker

Ayunli (ah yung' li)—Dance leader, first in the dance

Gahistiski (gah hees tee' skee)—Peacemaker

Galilahi (gah lee' lah hee)—Gentle, amiable, attractive

Gateya (gah tay' yah)*—Frighten it away

Gatitla (gah tee' tlah)*—They run to her

Gayini (gah yee' nee)*—Leading by the hand

Kamama (ka mah' mah)—Butterfly

Nakwisi (nah' kwee see)—Star

Nundayeli (nung dah yay' lee)—Midday sun

Salali (sah lah' lee)—Squirrel

Sinasta (seen ah' stah)—Expert

Tayanita (tah yah nee' tah)—Young beaver

Tsungani (tsoon gah' nee)—Excels all others

Ulskasti (ools kah' stee)—Fearless, independent

CHOCTAW—*Mississippi and Alabama*

There is no definite rule for placing the accent in the Choctaw language. Generally speaking, each syllable in a word is given equal stress.

Achukma (ah chook mah)—Purity

Achunanchi (ah choon ahn chee)—Perseverance

55

Ahah ahni (ah hah ah nee)—Careful, solicitous
Aiokpanchi (I oke pahn chee)—Welcome
Akomachi (ah ko mah chee)—Sweet
Apelachi (ah pay lah chee)—A helper
Bishkoko (beesh ko ko)—Red-headed woodpecker
Foe bilishke (foe bee leesh kay)—Honey-bee
Hobachi (ho bah chee)—Echo
Holitopa (ho lee toe pah)—Pearl
Ilatomba (ee lah tome bah)—Prudence
Nishkin halupa (neesh keen hah loo pah) Eagle-
    eyed (sharp-eyed)
Okshulba (oke shool bah)—Honeysuckle
Oktalonli (oke tah lone lee)—Blue-eyed
Yukpa (yook pah)—Merry
Yukpa shahli (yook pah shah lee)—Jolly
Yushbonuli (yoosh bo noo lee)—Curly-headed

CREEK—*Alabama and Georgia*

The meanings of some of these terms are unknown, but as
they are personal names in common use among these Indians
they are included.

Asihmi (ass ih' mi)*—"To give up"
Fulhaki (ful hah' kee)*—"They returned from
    the enemies"
Nahiyeli (nah hee yay' li)*—"Dancing" (as a
    babe is danced up and down)
Sihane (see hah' neh)*—"The enemy gets close
    enough to quarrel with them"
Teakfulichi (tee ak fool i' chee)—"To follow"

Tibai (tee bah' ee)*—"To add to" (child added to family)
Wilagwekhchi (wi lah gweh' khchi)—"A scout"
Mahoyi (mah ho' yi)*—Meaning unknown
Selani (seh lah' ni)*—Meaning unknown
Sindi (sin' di)*—Meaning unknown
Sipka (seep' kuh)*—Meaning unknown
Wani (wah' ni)*—Meaning unknown
Wilti (wil' ti)*—Meaning unknown
Chuli (choo' li)—Pine tree
Fuswa (foos' wah)—Bird
Fuschati (foos chah' ti)—Redbird
Hoktuchi chutki (hoke too' chi choot' ki)—Little girl
Takfolupa (tack fo loo' pah)—Butterfly

HIDATSA—*North Dakota*

Apitsa (ah peet' sah)—Crane
Apoksha (ah poke' sha)—Jewel
Imaksidi (ee mahk see' dee)—Lark
Madadaka (mah' dah dah kah)—Snowbird
Makhupa (mah khoo pah')—Spirit-creature
Maishu (mah ee shoo')—Golden eagle
Matsu (maht' soo)—Cherry
Miakaza (mee ah kah' zah)—Young woman
Mitskapa (meets kah' pah)—Rose
Sakagawea (sah kah gah' way ah)*—Bird woman

DAKOTA OR SIOUX—*North and South Dakota, Minnesota, Montana, Wyoming, Nebraska*

The names starred in this list were taken from old Indian reservation payrolls.

Akikhoka (ah kee' kho kah)—One who is skilful

Chantesuta (chahng tay' soo tah)—To be firm of heart

Chanteyukan (chahng tay' yoo kahng)—To have a kind heart; benevolent

Chumani (choo' mah nee)—Dewdrops

Hapanwin (hah pahn ween)*—Second daughter

Hinhanwaste (heen hahn wah stay)*—Pretty Owl

Kimimela (kee mee' may lah)—Butterfly

Makhpiyato (makh pee' yah toe)—The blue sky

Makawin (mah kah ween)*—Earth woman

Owanyakena (o wahn yah kay nah)*—Pretty

Paji (pah jee)*—Yellow hair

Tanyanmaniwin (tahn yahn mah nee ween)*—Woman that walks pretty

Wahihi (wah hee hee)*—Soft snow

Wakasansan (wah kah' sahng sahng)—Snowbird

Wakichonza (wah kee' chon zah)—One who determines or decides; a leader

Wakishaka (wah kee' shah kah)—One who never tires; indefatigable

Wanyecha (wahng yay' chah)—Firefly

Waokiya (wah oh' kee yah)—One who commands

Wapike (wah' pee kay)—One who is fortunate

58

Wastewayakapiwin (wah stay wah yah kah pee ween)*—Woman who is pretty to look at
Wawidake (wah wee' dah kay)—A ruler
Wawokiye (wah wo' kee yay)—One who helps
Wichincha (wee cheeng' chah)—Girl
Wichaka (wee chah' kah)—To be true
Winona (wee' no nah)—First born, if a daughter
Wiwasteka (wee' wah stay kah)—Beautiful woman
Woape (wo' ah pay)—Hope
Wogan (wo' ghahng)—Snowdrift
Wokiyapi (wo' kee yah pee)—Peace
Wokiziye (wo' kee zee yay)—A healer
Woksape (wo' ksah pay)—Wisdom
Woohiye (wo' oh hee yay)—Victory
Wowachintanka (wo' wah cheeng tahng kah)—Patience
Wowashake (wo' wah shah kay)—Strength
Wowichada (wo' wee chah dah)—Faith
Wowichake (wo' wee chah kay)—Truth
Wowitan (wo' wee tahng)—Honor
Zhonta (zhong' tah)—Trustworthy
Zitkana (zee tkah nah)*—Bird
Zitkalaska (zee tkah' lah skah)—White bird pure
Zitkatanka (zee tkah' tahng kah)—Blackbird

OSAGE—*Missouri, Kansas, Oklahoma*
Mina (mee' nah)—Elder sister
Niabi (nee' ah bee)—Fawn (one that is spared by the hunter)

Tewauh (tay wah uh)*—Buffalo Woman
Wihe (wee' hay)—Younger sister

PAWNEE—*Nebraska*

Apikatos (ah pee' kah tos)—Antelope
Chowat (cho waht')—Little girl
Irari (ee rah' ree)—Friend
Koru (ko' roo)—Moon
Lihtakats (leeh' tah kahts)—Eagle
Likutski (lee koots' kee)—Bird

CROW—*Montana*

Arakashe (ah rah kah' shay)—Sunlight
Asirik (ah see' reek)—Bud (of a tree or flower)
Bitskipe (beets kee pay')—Rosebud
Dakakchia (dah kah chee' ah)—Red-headed wood-
    pecker
Dakakshuak (dah kah shoo' ahk)—Bluebird
Manake (mah nah' kay)—My child
Popate (po pah' teh)—Owl

NEZ PERCE (nay per say')—*Idaho, Oregon*

Hatiya (hah' tee yah)—Wind
Ilakawit (ee lah kah' weet)—Light
Khastiyo (khah stee' yo)—Star
Tekut (teh' kut)—Golden-winged woodpecker
Tilipe (tee lee' peh)—Fox
Watsamyus (wah tsahm' yoos)—Rainbow
Weptesh (wep' tesh)—Eagle

Wisaskesit (wee sahs keh′ seet)*—The clouds
shade the sun
Witalu (wee′ tah loo)—Dove

ASSINIBOIN—*Province of Alberta, Canada, and
the State of Montana*
Chiwintku (chee weent′ koo)—Daughter
Hawi (hah wee′)—Moon
Koda (ko dah′)—Friend
Shunkashana (shoonk ah shah′ nah)—Red fox
Titkana (teet kah′ nah)—Bird
Tokana (toe kah′ nah)—Gray fox
Wakomohiza (wah ko mo′ hee zah)—Maize
Wamindi (wah meen dee′)—Eagle
Wichapi (wee chah′ pee)—Star

BLACKFOOT—*The Province of Alberta, Canada,
and the State of Montana*
Akima (ah kee′ mah)—Woman
Aponi (ah po′ nee)—Butterfly
Isakimi (ee sah′ kee me)—Sister
Kakatos (kah kah′ tos)—Star
Kiniks (kee neeks′)—Rosebud
Nituna (nee too′ nah)—My daughter

PIEGAN—*Belong to the Blackfoot tribe*
Aksutamaki (ahk soo tah′ mah kee)*—Good-
leader woman
Aksuwataneki (ahk soo wah tahn′ nay kee)*—
Shield woman

Iksuyawauka (eek soo yah wah' ooh kah)*—
Wades in water
Ipisoaki (ee pee so' ah kee)*—Morning-star woman
Kaiyetscheaki (kah ee yates chay' ah kee)*—Sings
in the air
Natosaki (nah toe' sah kee)*—Sun woman
Nitowaakia (nee toe wah ah' kee ah)*—Medicine
woman
Piksaki (peek sah' kee)*—Hawk woman
Pinatoyaki (pee nah toe yah' kee)*—Fisher woman
Pitaki (pee' tah kee)*—Eagle woman
Pokunaki (poke oon' ah kee)*—Pearl woman
Sinupaki (see noo pah' kee)*—Fox woman

GOSIUTE—*Western Utah and eastern Nevada.
Belong to the Ute tribe*
Kanagwana (kah' nah gwah nah)—Evening prim-
rose
Komu (ko' moo)—Indian corn
Kusiakendzip (koo' see ah ken dzip)—Arrowroot
Miropampi (mee' ro pahm pee)—Buttercup
Pasagwip (pah' sah gwip)—Sweet Cicely
Pawapi (pah' wah pee)—Red cedar
Tiabi (tee' ah bee)—Wild rose
Tibawara (tee' bah wah rah)—Pinon pine
Toiyadisas (toy' yah dee sahs)—Golden aster

ARAPAHO—*Wyoming, Colorado, Oklahoma*
Bachewishe (bah chay wee' shay)—Red willow

62

Nihanaina (nee hah nah′ ee nah)—Yellow flower
Suskuito (soos koo′ ee toe)—Ground sparrow

ZUNI—*New Mexico*

Akyamoni (ah′ kyah mo ni)—Garnet
Kohakwa (ko′ hah kwah)—White-shell bead
Kyatsiki (kyat′ see kee)—Little girl; daughter
Kyakyali (kya′ kya li)—Eagle
Neshapakoya (nesh′ ah pah ko yah)—Dove
Ohapa (oh′ hah pah)—Bee
Okshiko (oke′ she ko)—Rabbit
Omatsupa (oh′ mah tsoo pah)—Sunflower
Onaaway (oh′ nah ah way)—Blossoms
Shohoita (sho′ hoy ta)—Deer
Tawya (taw′ yah)—Maize, corn
Tehya (tay′ hyah)—Precious
Thliakwa (thlee′ ah kwah)—Turquoise
Tona (toe′ nah)—Turkey
Tonashi (toe′ nah she)—Badger
Tsana (tsah′ nah)—Little
Tsawya (tsaw′ yah)—Pretty; bright
Yachune (yatch′ oo nay)—Moon
Yaktosha (yahk′ to shah)—Beautiful
Yashi (yah′ she)—Pine squirrel
Yatokya (ya′ to kyah)—Sun

NAVAHO—*Arizona, New Mexico, southeastern Utah*

Bilatqahi (bee lat′ kha hee)—Flower
Bitsos (beet sos′)—Down-feather

Datsa (da′ tsa)—Mistletoe
Doli (doll′ lee)—Bluebird
Dolihlchi (doe′ lihl chee)—Red-breasted bluebird
Kalugi (kah lug′ ee)—Butterfly
Shandin (shan dine)—Sunlight
Sotso (so′ tso)—Morning star
Soyazhe (so ya′ zhay)—Little star
Tsisna (tsis na′)—Bee
Zahalani (za hah la′ nee)—Mockingbird
Zahalzhin (za′ hahl zhine)—Sparrow (English sparrow)

NOOTKA—*Vancouver Island, British Columbia*
Aptsina (ahpts′ ee nah)—Abalone shell
Chiishkale (chee ish′ kah lay)—Kingfisher
Chukudabi (chuck oo′ dah bi)—Sparrow
Koushin (ko′ oo shin)—Raven
Kwalis (kwahl′ iss)—Crane
Mawi (mah′ wee)—Red Pine
Qishqishi (kish kish′ ee)—Bluejay
Totopichus (to to pi chus′)—Cottontail rabbit
Tuchi (too′ chee)—East wind
Tsutsutsid (tsoo tsoo′ tsid)—Chipmunk
Yoati (yo′ ah ti)—North wind

HAIDA—*Queen Charlotte Islands, British Columbia, and southern Alaska*
Kaecho (kah ay′ chow)—Star
Kalgahlina (kahl′ gahl ee′ nah)—Abalone shell

64

Kaltsida (kahl tsi' dah)— Crow
Skahio (skah hee ow')—Robin

Reindeer Totem

Camp Names

CHEROKEE

Adahi (ah dah' hee)—In the woods; forest place
Ahaluna (ah hah loo' nah)—Lookout place
Amadahi (ah mah dah' hee)—Forest water
Amaiyulti (ah mah ee yool' tee)—Water side; near the water
Amuganasta (ahm ooga nah' stah)—Sweetwater
Ayeliyu adahi (ah yale ee' yoo ah dah' hee)—In the heart (middle) of the woods
Elitsehi (ay leet say' hee)—Green meadow; verdant fields
Gatiyi (gah tee' yee)—Town house; (tribal dance and council house)
Gatusi (gah too' see)—In the mountain
Inagei (ee nah gay' ee)—In the wilderness
Natsihi (naht see' hee)—In the pines
Saluyi (sah loo' yee)—In the thicket
Talahi (tah lah' hee)—In the oaks; oak forest
Tsiskwahi (tsees kwah' hee)—Bird place

Unaliyi (oon ah lee' yee)—Place of friends
Unilawisti (oon eel ah wee' stee)—Council place
Untalulti (oon tah lool' tee)—On the bank of
the lake
Ustanali (oo stahn ah' lee)—Rock ledge
Wahiliyi (wah hee lee' yee)—Eagle place
Yanahi (yah nah' hee)—Bear place

CHIPPEWA

Agaming (ah gah ming')—On the shore
Anokiwaki (ah no ki wah' ki)—Hunting-ground
Anwebewin (ahn' web eh win')—Rest; quietness
Chickagami (chick' ah gah mi')—By the lake
Chigakwa (chi gah kwah')—Near the forest
Manakiki (mah' nah ki ki')—Maple-forest
Mitigwaking (mi' ti gawh king')—In the woods
Nawakwa (nah wah kwah')—In the midst of the
forest
Nissaki (nis sah ki')—At the foot of the mountain
Nopiming (no pim ing')—In the woods
Wakitatina (wah ki tah ti' nah)—On the hilltop
Wasabinang (wah' sah bi nahng')—Outlook; at
the place of looking

DAKOTA

Chanyata (chahng yah' tah)—At the woods
Tingtata (teeng tah' tah)—On the prairie
Waziyata (wah zee yah' tah)—At the pines

DELAWARE

Shankitunk (shahn' kee toonk)—Woody place
Meniolagamika (may nee oh lah gah mee' kah)—
Pleasant enclosure

MIAMI

Chipkahki oongi (cheep kah' kee oon ge)—Place
of roots

CREEK

Ikan-hilusi (ee' kon hee loo' see)—Beautiful land
Tula-hilusi (too' lah hee loo' see)—Beautiful country
Ukhusi-kunhi (ook hoo' see koon' hee)—Crooked
lake

CHOCTAW

Aiowata (i oh wut' ah)—Hunting ground
Hotak-aiukli (ho' tahk i ook' lee)—Beautiful lake
Nan-okweli (nahn' ok way' lee)—Fishing place
Ok-aiyoka (oke' i yo' kah)—Beautiful water
Tiak foka (tee' ahk fo' kah)—Piney region

NATICK

Wusapinuk (wuh sa' pin uk)—Bank (of a river)

Deer Totem

Club Names

MOHAWK

Otyokwa (ote yo' kwah)—A group or body of persons forming a single fellowship

NATICK

Mukkinneunk (muk kin' ne unk)—A gathering; an assembly

POWHATAN

Netoppew (ne' top pew)—Friends

Cheskchamay (chesk' cha may)—All friends

NARRAGANSETT

Nowetompatimmin (no we tom pat' im min)—We are friends

Wetomachick (we' to ma chick)—Friends

Crane Totem

Names Suitable for Country Homes or Bungalows

CHEROKEE

Akwenasa (ah kwain' ah sah)—My home

Kultsa te adahi (kult sah' tay ah dah' he)—House in the woods

Watuhiyi (wah too he' ye)—Beautiful place

68

CHOCTAW

Aboha afoha (ah bo' hah ah fo' ha)—House of rest

Aboha hanta (ah bo' hah hahn' tah)—House of peace

Aiyukpa (i yoo' kpah)—Happy place

Ayataia (i yah ty' ah)—Resting place

Oka-balama (o' kah bah lah' mah)—Sweetwater

POWHATAN

Machacammac (match a kam' mak)—Great house

Wahchesao (watch ee sah' o)—Bird's nest

Yohacan (yo hah' kan)—House

NARRAGANSETT

Ponewhush (po' nee whush)—Lay down your burdens

Weekan (we e' kan)—It is sweet

Yokowish (yo ko' wish)—Do lodge here

NATICK

Wetuomuck (weh' too oh muck)—At home

Wolf Totem

Boat Names

CHOCTAW

Chilantakoba (chee lahn tah ko bah)—Pelican

Oka hushi (oke ah hoo she)—Waterfowl

Fichik hika (fee cheek hee kah)—Flying star

BLACKFOOT
Maniski (mah nee' skee)—Water lizard
Miesa (mee ay' sah)—Fish duck

ARAPAHO
Awuth nakuwee (ah wooth' nah koo' way ay)—
White-nosed duck
Babithinahe (bah bee theen' ah hay)—Little red-
winged bird

DAKOTA
Tamahe (tah' mah hay)—Pike
Witawata (wee' tah wah tah)—Ship
Witko (wee tko')—Dogfish

DELAWARE
Kopohan—Sturgeon
Hurissameck—Catfish

ASSINIBOIN
Makhaska (mah khah' skah)—Swan
Patkasha (paht kah' shah)—Turtle

ONONDAGA
Anokie (ah no' kee ay)—Water Rat
Onaton (oh nah' tone)—Water Snake

NOOTKA
Bishawih (bee shah' wih)—Black cod
Hahashid (hah' hah sheed)—Red cod
Qalal (khal' ahl)—Sea gull
Haqadish (hah kha' deesh)—Sea lion

70

Hinikoas (hee nee' ko ass)—Dog salmon
Hitsiwunni (hee' tsee wun nee)—Porpoise
Kalahlchu (kah lahl' choo)—Flounder
Shuyuhl (shoo yuhl')—Halibut
Tichuk (tee' chuck)—Sea Otter
Yacha (yah' chah)—Dogfish

HAIDA
Chanskagit (chahn' skah git)—Blackfish
Kahada (kah' hah dah)—Dogfish

POWHATAN
Acomtan (a' kom tan)—Boat
Coiahgwus (koy' ah gwus)—Gull
Cuppatoan (kup pah toe' an)—Sturgeon
Namaske (na' mask)—Fish
Potawaugh (po' tah waw)—Porpoise
Tatamaho (tah tah mah' ho)—Garfish

Frog Totem

A few Musical Indian Tribal Names that might Serve for Bungalows, Country Seats, or Boats

Abnaki (ahb nah' ki)
Alibamu (ali bah' moo)
Apache (a pach' ee)
Arapaho (ah rap' ah ho)
Bellacoola (bel lah kool' ah)
Catawba (kah taw' bah)
Cayuga (ky you' ga)
Chastacosta (chas ta cost' ah)
Cherokee (cher' oh kee)
Cheyenne (shy en')
Chickahominy (chick a hom' i ny)
Chickasaw (chick' i saw)
Chilkat (chil' kat)
Chimariko (chim ah ree' ko)
Chinook (chin ook')
Chippewa (chip' pe way)
Choctaw (chock' taw)
Cochiti (ko chi tee')
Comanche (ko man' chee)
Cree (kree)
Croatan (kro' ah tan)
Haida (hide' ah)
Hidatsa (hid aht' sah)
Kalispel (kal' iss pel)
Kickapoo (kick' ah poo)
Kiowa (ky' oh wah)
Koasati (ko ah sah' ti)

Kutenai (koot' en eye)
Kwakiutl (kwahk' i ootl)
Maidu (my' doo)
Maricopa (mah ree ko' pah)
Micmac (mick' mack)
Mohave (mo ha' vay)
Mohawk (mo' hawk)
Mohegan (mo hee' gan)
Munsee (mun' see)
Narraganset (nar ra gan' set)
Navaho (nahv' ah ho)
Nootka (noot' kah)
Omaha (oh' mah ha)
Oneida (oh ny' dah)
Onondaga (oh non dah' gah)
Osage (oh' sage)
Ottawa (ot' tah wah)
Pamunkey (pah mun' key)
Passamaquoddy (pah sah mah quod' dy)
Pawnee (paw nee')
Penobscot (pen ob' skot)
Piegan (pee' gan)
Potawatomi (pot a waht' oh mi)
Powhatan (pow ha tan')
Salish (say' lish)
Santiam (san' ti am)
Seminole (sem i no' li)
Seneca (sen' ek ah)
Shawnee (shaw nee')

Shinnecock (shin' nee cock)
Shoshoni (sho sho' nee)
Sioux (soo)
Tonkawa (tonk' ah way)
Tuscarora (tusk ah ro' rah)
Wichita (wich' i taw)
Winnebago (win nee bay' go)
Wyandot (wy' an dot)
Yakima (yah' ki mah)

Some Indian Terms Useful as Mottoes

NARRAGANSETT

  Kowaunkamish (ko waunk' ah mish)—My service
    to you

  Wetompatitea (wee tom pa' ti tee ah)—Let us
    make friends

  Wunnishaunta (wun nish awn' tah)—Let us agree

IROQUOIS

  Chiakong (chee ah kong)—Do what thou canst

DELAWARE

  Wichingen (wee cheen gain)—To help along.

  Elgithin (ale gee theen)—To be worthy

Merman Totem

74

BOOKS CONSULTED

Baraga, Frederic. A Dictionary of the Otchipwe Language, explained in English. Montreal, 1878.

Byington's Choctaw Dictionary, edited by J. R. Swanton and H. S. Halbert. Washington, 1915.

Chamberlin, Ralph V. The Ethno-botany of the Gosiute Indians of Utah. Lancaster, Pa., 1911.

Culin, Stewart. Games of the North American Indians. Washington, 1907.

Curtis, Edward S. The North American Indian. New York, 1907-1916.

Dunn, J. P. True Indian Stories. Cedar Rapids, Iowa, 1909.
Massacres of the Mountains. New York, 1886.

Franciscan Fathers—A Vocabulary of the Navaho Language. St. Michaels, Arizona, 1912.

Handbook of American Indians, edited by F. W. Hodge. Washington, 1907-1910.

Hayden, F. V. Contributions to the Ethnography and Philology of the Indian Tribes of the Missouri Valley. Philadelphia, 1862.

Hough, Walter. The Methods of Fire-making. Washington, 1892.
The Hopi Indians. Cedar Rapids, Iowa, 1915.

Matthews, Washington. Ethnography and Philology of the Hidatsa Indians. Washington, 1877.

Mooney, James. Myths of the Cherokee. Washington, 1900.

Rand, Silas Tertius. Dictionary of the Language of the Micmac Indians. Halifax, 1888.

Riggs, S. R. Grammar and Dictionary of the Dakota Language, collected by members of the Dakota Mission. Washington, 1851.

Strachey, William. The Historie of Travaile into Virginia Britannia; written in 1611. London, 1849.

Trumbull, J. H. Natick Dictionary. Washington, 1903.

Williams, Roger. Key to the [Narragansett] Indian Language. Providence, 1827.

Zeisberger's Indian Dictionary, translated by Eben Norton Horsford. Cambridge, Mass., 1887.

Kingfisher Totem

Good Books to Read

Curtis, Edward S.   Indian Days of Long Ago.
    Yonkers-on-Hudson, New York, 1915
    In The Land of The Head-Hunters.   Yonkers-
    on-Hudson, New York, 1915.

Dunn, J. P.   True Indian Stories.   Cedar Rapids,
    Iowa, 1908.

Fletcher, Alice C.   Indian Story and Song from
    North America.   Boston, 1900.

Grinnell, G. B.   The Punishment of the Stingy and
    Other Indian Stories.   New York, 1901.

Handbook of American Indians, Bulletin 30 of the
    Bureau of American Ethnology, edited by F.
    W. Hodge.

> (This book contains articles and notes on all the In-
> dians studied up to 1907. It is no longer available for
> distribution by the Bureau, but may be consulted, to-
> gether with all other Bureau pnblications, in the libraries
> of all State universities and in the public libraries of the
> larger cities, or it may be purchased from the Superin-
> tendent of Documents, Government Printing Office,
> Washington, D. C., at $3.00 for the two volumes.)

Hough, Walter, The Hopi Indians.   Cedar Rapids,
    1915.

Jackson, Helen Hunt.   A Century of Dishonor.
    New York, 1881.

Jenks, Albert E.   The Childhood of Ji-shib the
    Ojibwa.   Madison, Wisconsin, 1900.

La Flesche, Francis. The Middle Five. Boston, 1901.

Lipps, Oscar H. The Navaho. Cedar Rapids, 1909.

Lummis, C. F. A New Mexico David and Other Stories and Sketches of the Southwest. New York, 1891.

The Man Who Married The Moon and Other Pueblo Indian Folk-stories. New York, 1894.

The King of The Broncos and Other Stories of New Mexico. New York, 1897.

McLaughlin, James. My Friend the Indian. Boston, 1910.

Ober, Fred A. Tommy Foster's Adventures among the Southwest Indians. Philadelphia, 1901.

Saunders, Charles F. The Indians of the Terraced Houses. New York and London, 1912.

Skinner, Alanson, The Indians of Greater New York. Cedar Rapids, 1915.

Wilson, Gilbert L. Goodbird, the Indian. New York, Chicago, and Toronto, 1914.

THE END